An Introduction to the AMIF / MAMIF

*Management Model
Based on
Learning Theories
and
Models*

Dr. Mahmoud Ajami

Tanin-e-Kherad Co.
(Echo of Wisdom)

June 2017

Copyright © 2017

All rights reserved.

ISBN: 978-1544636764

INTRODUCTION

By ever increasing roles of organizations, as a leverage point in development of human societies, the experts have become more and more interested in organizational excellence.

Scientific management achievement since 1900 and the recognition of the roles of managers in organizational excellence, have made it clear that, upgrading of the knowledge of managers is essential for betterment of the organization and hence, for improvement of the human societies in general.

Tanin-e-Kherad Consulting Company (TeKCo), concentrating its activities on human resource development has put its effort on introducing leadership and management as independent organizational thought and task and in this respect has succeeded in training capable and knowledgeable leaders and managers in various organizations. A group of empowered leaders and managers who could bring about changes to their organizations and lead them into a state at which, development of human abilities and continuous improvement of organizational relationship could become possible and a learning organization could be shaped.

To create changes in organizational leadership and management, TeKCo has employed a special model known as MAMIF[1]. This model consists of seven stages and has been applied during the last twelve years in more than 20 well reputed companies in Iran successfully. The four-period version of this model, known as AMIF[2], is used for creation of shared vision among the senior managers of a company and preparation of strategic plan and strategy map for the company, based on the created shared vision.

---

[1] Management through AMIF
[2] Ajami's Managerial Intervention Framework

The Evolutionary Process of AMIF/MAMIF Models

It is noteworthy to know that, the AMIF Model and its complementary version known as MAMIF model are both developed by the founder of TeKCo, Dr. Mahmoud Ajami and at the first were applied on three Power Generation Management Companies in Iran (Sep. 1998 – Dec. 2000). The validity of these models has been certified by TAVANIR Holding Company, the most authorized body in Iran Electric Power Industry (EPI). Later on they were also applied on several Regional Electric Companies in Iran. First implementation of AMIF model outside of Iran electric power industry was in Bandar Imam Petrochemical Company (BIPC) and later on other petrochemical companies in Iran. The results of all these experiences have been debated in a special session, held by the authorities of the Fourth International Management Conference–Tehran - Iran (Dec. 2006) and have received the approval of the technical board of the above referred conference as a successful experience in management and also has been rewarded a note of gratitude from the chairman of the Board of that Conference.

The path which led the research to AMIF/MAMIF models

This work has been initiated when the management of Iran Electric Power Industry decided to re-evaluate the performance of the power generation management companies. The author then was asked to carry out a thorough study about the ways of improving the management performance of these companies through upgrading the skill of their managers to the extent that, they could work in a competitive private organization environment as it was decided by TAVANIR ,Holding company, to privatize the electric power generation sector. Therefore, a proposal was submitted to TAVANIR and upon the approval of it the work has started. The approach in the proposal has based on action research basis, therefore with such a background a framework consisting of four stages of promotion of knowledge and practice of management has been developed. The second major step was to deal with the cultural and ideological differences that exists between Eastern and Western Nations of the world and blocks the way entering into domain of collective thinking. Fortunately, based on managerial consultancy background of the author, an approach of consultancy was developed to overcome the cultural barriers. The approach was then named as "Caravan Balad-e-Rah (CBR)"[3]. That means instead of making a group of people to follow a path, moving with them through the path.

---

[3] Caravan Balad-e-Rah (CBR): in ancient time, when a caravan wanted to cross a desert, it had to employ a person who knew the safe way through the desert and knew the dangers of wilderness, so he could guide caravan through the desert safely. Such a person was named as "Balad-e-Rah" and its approach was named, by the author, as "Caravan Balad-e-Rah" and in brief, CBR. The main reason for such a nomination is the similarity between the management approach in traditional management system of most eastern countries and wilderness of a desert. You cannot cross it just by having a fixed address. Everything changes by changing the direction of wind, hills turn into valleys and valleys into flat lands or even hill. Crossing desert without CBR means taking the risk of getting lost and facing death.

As a consequence, at the end of these four stages the following results were observed:
- The level of sharing among the participants increased.
- Putting forward new ideas, and concluding their discussions on each issue, a common beliefs and understanding developed, among the participants.
- A common process of decision-making was also developed.
- Senior managers gradually came together as members of a team in scientific sense.
- Senior managers reached to systems thinking as an approach of thinking in management and as a managerial language.

As a general result it has been found that, one can not imply the method of management common in the western countries in the Eastern part of the world, unless so tailored to suit the socio - cultural beliefs of those nations. The main achievement of CBR approach of consultancy is the fact that, it does not solve the problem of management of organization, but help the managerial team to cooperate for surfacing the problem first, then solving them by themselves. Therefore, in CBR approach the consultant moves through the path with all members of the caravan, instead of telling them that is the path you may cross it if you wish so.

Later on, the managerial intervention framework was developed, now known as AMIF. Getting experienced with AMIF performance and surfacing complementary needs of organizations, the author gradually developed the "Management through AMIF", now known as MAMIF Model of management.

The principles on which the AMIF/MAMIF is Based

The consultancy approach of this model is based on "Action Research" doctrine and it was developed as an attempt to create a framework to facilitate, observe and measure the possibility of sharing among a group of individuals, through tactical interventions. In this approach the consultant plays the role of an interventionist throughout the whole length of consultancy.

The AMIF Model has it's emphasize on generative learning. This Model emphasizes on co-thinking which is crystallized in process of "sharing". Therefore, it stands on the principles that;

- Every activity should have a theoretical background and vice versa (Principle of T&O).
- Co-thinking is indispensable element of this model through "sharing" process.
- Systems thinking is as a manner of thinking for management and leadership, and participants get acquainted with it, and learn how to practice it.
- Mental model alignment is as a base for formation of a learning team.
- Shared vision of the managers team is created in a continuous movement and get acquainted with the conceptual and executable models.

Implementation Process of AMIF

AMIF is normally executed at senior management Level of an organization. The managers, together with consultant, form a caravan who decides to design and define certain goals and destination and start to move towards them for which they have prepared a long-term plan while they are determined to shape the future of their organization according to that plan.

The consultant starts its movement not as the leader of the group but as an informed person (Guide) who knows the way of Caravan to the destination set for the organization. As the movement of the "Caravan" proceeds, the consultant, without interfering with the decision of the managers, equips them with necessary information about the management theories and models that can be used by them for better organizational development. The consultant makes sure that, all the members of Caravan are participating in the general movement of the Caravan and their participation is based on scientific principles of management. In other words they are bonded to a set framework. During this movement towards the organizational development, three written reports will be prepared by senior managers, as caravan members, in which major obstacles on the way of "Caravan" will be referred to and selected solutions of overcoming these obstacles are discussed.

Normally, AMIF is executed in four stages with each stage lasting for about six months. Each month will be ended with a five hours session in the company in which the model is implemented and the outcome of execution of the model is discussed at the presence of the consultant. The consultant without interfering in decision making of managers is present for helping them for better implementation of their managerial duties and skills.

The four stages of AMIF are shown schematically in Fig. 1 and each stage is explained as follows:

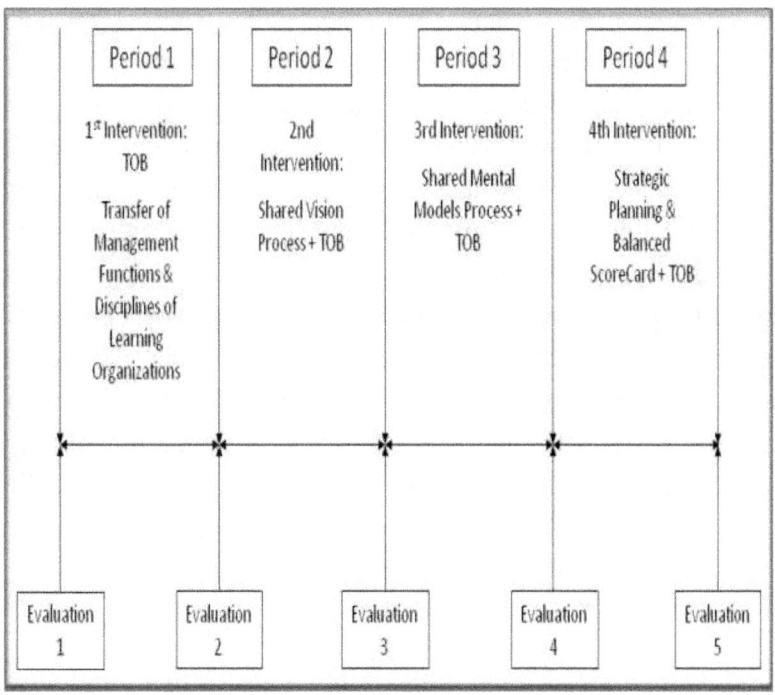

Stage (1): Transfer of Basics: Theories and Models (TOB)

The main objective, followed by this stage, is creation of a basis for provision of necessary management knowledge and vision among the participants and prepares them for their future activities. In this stage, five classical management functions, the related models and the five disciplines of the learning organizations are presented through conferences and workshops which are put forward by participating managers under direct supervision of the consultant. This method of transfer of the basic theories and models is adapted to ensure that, while the relative knowledge of managers is upgraded, they come to this very important conclusion that management of an organization is a vital task and a key factor to organizational success and has to be founded on a sound theories and models driven from those theories.

Stage (2): Shared Vision Process (SVP+TOB)

The movement in this stage is oriented toward creation of a shared vision among the senior managers for the future of their organization. The process of shaping a phrase as a general statement of vision will be accomplished through the skill of dialogue.

The result of this process will be published in a report under the title of [shared vision of the senior Manager (first version)] which will be released at the end of this stage. In this report, the process and the general statement of shared vision and also the related guidelines and main actions which had to be taken are elaborated.

Stage (3): Shared Mental Models Process (SMMP+TOB)

Reaching to a shared vision becomes materialized when the mental models of those who are seeking or moving toward shared vision are aligned accordingly. Therefore, at this stage all attempts are made to align the mental models of the members and create new shared mental models aligned with shared vision and define the ways of achieving it. This vital process is followed through continuation of dialogues on various dimensions of shared vision and ways of its execution .At the end of this stage a report entitled, {shared vision of the senior Managers (second version)} will be also published.

Stage (4): Strategic Planning and Strategy Map (SP & BSC+TOB)

This stage of AMIF model is in fact the first step toward materialization of created shared vision and extension of it in all dimensions and levels of the organization to the extent that new ideas are evolved within the organization and are reflected in the strategic plan of the organization both quantitatively and qualitatively. At the end of this stage strategic plan and strategy map are developed. Within the context of them, the managers state the ways that they would lead the organization towards its strategic goals and define indices for evaluation of the progress and monitoring of movement of the organization in its path toward its set destination.

Organizational Management through the AMIF: A Seven-stage Model that is known as MAMIF

Upon completion of the fourth stage of AMIF Model, the strategic plan of the organization and its strategy map are prepared based on shared vision of senior Managers. To complete this path which has an indispensable role in organizational learning, the seven-stage model known as MAMIF is developed. MAMIF stands for management through the AMIF. The activities of stages one through four of MAMIF are AMIF and at the fifth stage of MAMIF, operational plans, for all goals and objectives are prepared and at the 6th stage, annul budget is prepared. Provision of suitable terms and conditions for effective implementation of programs depends on systems thinking through which a feedback path to each stage becomes possible and the principle of "Close the Loop (or CTL)" and hence completing the process of learning is fulfilled. The main mission of stage seven of MAMIF is "Execution" which in turn provides the foundation for the next new cycle i.e. new vision and strategic plan of the organization. Figure 2 shows the various stages of MAMIF, in a new designed model, schematically.

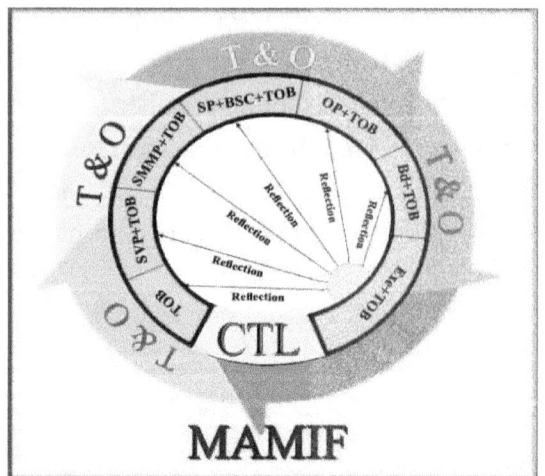

Fig. 2

Note: T&O stands for theory and operation which is the basic principle of each stage of MAMIF

Organizational Development and Excellence based on MAMIF model

There is no doubt that a deep rooted sustainable change in any organization would not become possible unless, organizational beliefs and personnel mental models are coordinated for favorable changes. Therefore, to meet this, after stage 4 and parallel to stages 5 and 6 [preparation of operational plans and annual budgets] of MAMIF, a new foundation for another movement will be laid down in the organization. It is a set of courses which will be implemented due to preferences of the senior managers. Figure 3 shows the set of courses in MAMIF model.

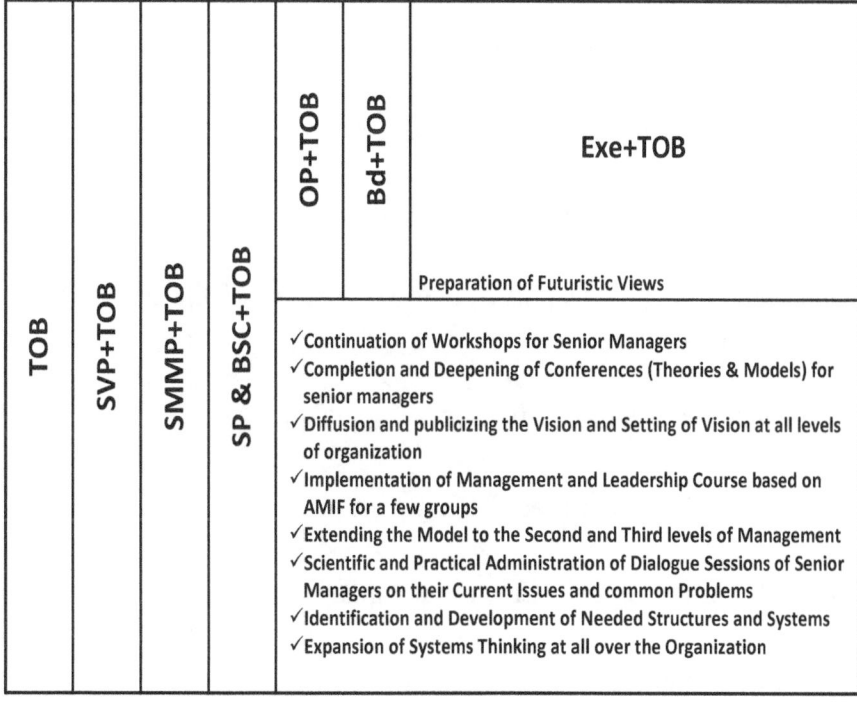

Fig. 3 Organizational Development and Excellence through MAMIF

Experiences with AMIF/MAMIF

Up to now AMIF/MAMIF models have been executed successfully in the following organizations in Iran:

- ✓ Neka Power Generation Management Company
- ✓ Tous Power Generation Management Company
- ✓ Semnan Regional Electric Company
- ✓ Bandar Imam Petrochemical Company (BIPC)
- ✓ Faravaresh Petrochemical Company
- ✓ Qom Power Generation Management Company
- ✓ Boo–Ali–Sina Petrochemical Company
- ✓ Department of Deputy for Power Affairs of the Ministry of Energy of Iran
- ✓ Shahid Tondgooyan Petrochemical Company
- ✓ Tehran Regional Electric Company
- ✓ Khorasan Regional Electric Company
- ✓ Fars Regional Electric Company
- ✓ Electric Distribution Company of the west of Tehran (Karaj District)

- ✓ Hormozgan Regional Electric Company

- ✓ Electric Distribution Company of the Southern Kerman Province

- ✓ Iran Power Grid Management Company (IGMC)

- ✓ Electric Distribution Company of Hormozgan Province

- ✓ Deputy for Human Resources and Productivity Improvement of TAVANIR Co.

- ✓ Kerman Regional Electric Company

- ✓ Tarasht Power Plant Operating Company

- ✓ Electric Distribution Company of Semnan Province

Examples of Comments passed on Soundness and Effectiveness of AMIF/MAMIF models by some Senior Managers and Experts of the Companies

"For me as a professor of management and as the Chairman of the International Management Conference, it is very pleasant to see that a management framework, developed and implemented by one of the Iranian scholars has received such an approval by different managing directors in different industries. On behalf of the Scientific and Industrial Committee Members of the Conference, I congratulate your success in articulating, developing and implementing your framework so successfully."

A part of letter of Dr. Mashayekhi, Professor on Management in Sharif University of Tehran and Chairman of International Management Conference, Dated 01 Jan. 2007

* * * * *

"I, as a manager, who has been working at high managerial level in the Electric Power Industry during last 14 years, would like to emphasize on the serious need of skill in mental coordination and sharing visions of managers of an organization.... The point that makes the achievement of this model distinguished among the other similar methods and models is the existence of such an entity of the model that makes the process of mental coordination and sharing visions easy to access."

A part of Letter written by Dr. Ahmadian, Deputy Minister of Energy in Electric Power Affairs, Dated 09 Dec. 2004

* * * * *

"During 38 years of my professional life, I had the opportunity of participating in various training courses and attending in different specialized seminars and conferences ....but, I have to state explicitly that, the effect of AMIF model on me and my colleagues was unique and quite different."

A part of letter written by Eng. Shaari Moghaddam the Managing Director of Bandar Imam Petrochemical Company (BIPC), dated Oct. 2004

* * * * *

"In our view, the most important achievement of this course was reaching to a collective learning, through which, a new horizon has been emerged for senior managers of our company and we do hope that, by extending this approach, team learning covers all levels of our organization to a state that we aim.

A part of letter of Eng. Fakhr-e-Nabavi, the Managing Director of Fars Regional Electric Company, Dated 05 Jul. 2004

* * * * *

Assuredly, the AMIF, management improvement course, has to be considered as the most prominent movement resulted in this great achievement. The aforesaid course, launched with your scientific and practical guidance for the company's managers 4 years ago, which is now expanded to all staff, has certainly played a major and undeniable role in creating a strong field for greater performances for BIPC. Its first result was to excel BIPC, which has become revealed in the evaluations done by EFQM's European's assessors.

A part of letter written by Eng. Nejad Salim, the Managing Director of Bandar Imam Petrochemical Company (BIPC) on the occasion of receiving EFQM certificate of Excellence from OQS Company Dated 18 Dec. 2006

* * * * *

"The management model of MAMIF has several features as follows:
   a. Creation of an insight for and a shared vision among members of group participating in the organizational reviving stage of MAMIF course.
   b. Co-thinking is an indispensable part of the Model, an issue which has a special place in development of all aspects of management science and it is through this stage of the Model that, the learning core is shaped in the organization.

c. Consultancy approach for this model is based on Action Research which may be referred to as the third feature of MAMIF model. The key role of consultancy in this model is in fact the spirit of the two previously referred issues. If omitted in implementation of the model then the model will be left as a useless corpse."

A part of comment passed by Eng. Fatah, the Managing Director of Tehran Regional Electric Company, on MAMIF model, in his address to the final session of strategic planning and design of strategy map of the company, Dated Jan. 2009

* * * * *

… Being acquainted with the scientific background of Dr. Ajami and his unique consultation approach as well as recommendation of several other managers of different organizations on the effectiveness of his approach, I have invited him to help our senior managers in their way toward establishment of a modern scientifically based management system, in our organization. The invitation was kindly accepted by him and the course of consultancy accomplished successfully and as a general wording of our organization vision we intended to become "the vanguard of green industry in Iran Electric Power Industry".

... We thank him for his valuable help and hope our company could be privileged by his precious consultancy continuously.
A part of Introduction, written by Eng. Majid Farahani, the Managing Director of Tarasht Power Plant Operating Company, Dated April 2012

* * * * *

Theory-and-Workshop course on Management & Leadership, based on AMIF

This Theory-and-Workshop course is designed to meet the need of those senior managers who wish to get acquainted with AMIF/MAMIF models and take advantage of these practical models for improvement of the performances of their company. In fact this course is designed to be substituted with stage one of AMIF model whereas Stages 2 and 3 of AMIF could be combined into a six-month course.

This course is designed on the basis of well known logic of "Theory and Operation (T&O)". Therefore, the course is also divided into two consecutive activities; learning theories and attending workshops. The course deals with management and leadership on the basis of AMIF model.

The course is implemented in two parts; in the first part, the basic theories of managements and leadership i.e. the five functions of classical management and the five disciplines of Peter Senge on learning organization are studied and their related models and laws are explained. In the second part of the course some workshops will be held for all theoretical issues presented in the first part and their related models are employed in a real world environment.

In the first part of the course, each participant is asked to prepare a presentation on his/her topic of interest which has been thought during the course and present it in a session. Each session takes four hours. In the session, after the presentation of each participant, the issue of the presentation will be also put on dialogue by other participants and various aspects of it will be further discussed to make sure that, a deep understanding of each issue is reached. At the end, the consultant sums up the session accordingly.

Finally, at the end of the course, in a concluding session, which may last more than three hours, an overview of the course will be presented by the consultant of the course and the content of the course will be evaluated by the participants. The course then will be concluded by a roadmap for the future of the organization.

Note: Since 2010 this course was held, in various companies, successfully. In fact it was the most requested course in recent years.

Theory-and-Workshop Course for Systems Thinking

We do recommend this course to those senior managers who are willing to have long-term planning for their organization. We think this course will provide them with the necessary background for development of their organizations on the basis of MAMIF model.

The main objective followed by implementation of this course is promotion of systems thinking as language of management and leadership, as well as its application in all activities of organization. No doubt, viewing an organization in its totality and wholeness for better understanding of the organizational behavior is an essential tool for organizational development.

This Theory-and-Workshop Course includes a preliminary section to introduce basic theories of systems thinking and their practice and would last 4 months. In the continuation of the course, the participants will get acquainted with the application of systems thinking in leadership and management and through practice and gaining experience they will reach to the level of skill that enable them to analyze the organization on the basis of iceberg-model and systems-archetypes. Therefore, through this course, the participants, accordingly, reach to the level of mastery that they begin to use systems thinking as a language and as a manner of thinking in management and leadership of the organization.

******

For further information about the contents of this Brochure, please get in touch with us via the following address:

info@tkherad.net

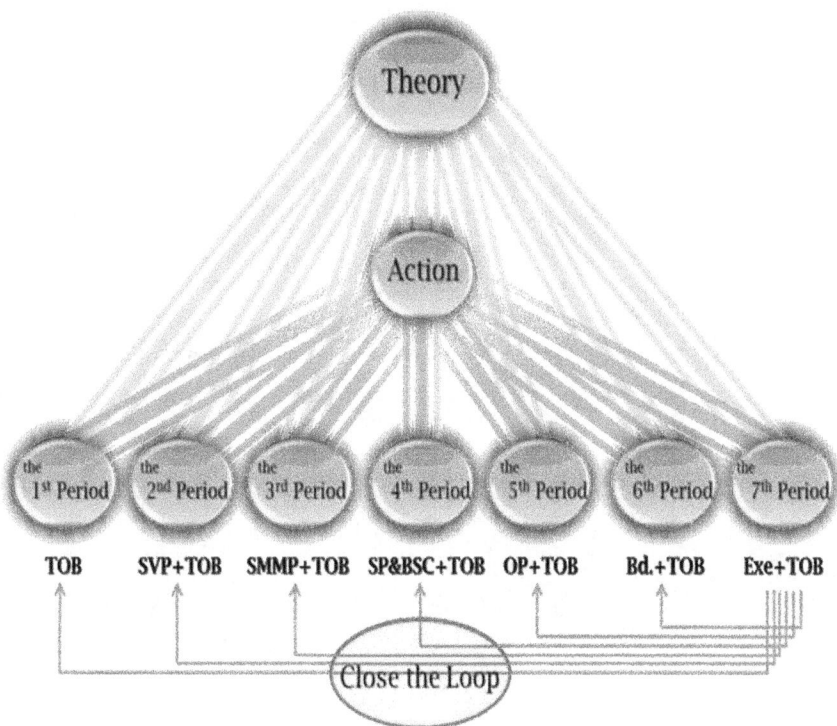

www.ingramcontent.com/pod-product-compliance
Lightning Source LLC
Chambersburg PA
CBHW061238180526
45170CB00003B/1348